February 11, 1988

To Mom
Love
Peter

MAINE

A Picture Book to Remember Her by

CRESCENT BOOKS
NEW YORK

Featuring the Photography of Julian Essam and Neil Sutherland
CLB 858
© 1986 Illustrations and text: Colour Library Books Ltd.,
Guildford, Surrey, England.
Text filmsetting by Acesetters Ltd., Richmond, Surrey, England.
All rights reserved.
Published 1986 by Crescent Books, distributed by Crown Publishers, Inc.
Printed and bound in Barcelona, Spain by Cronion, S.A.
ISBN 0 517 47805 6
g f e d c b a

If you were to take a helicopter ride along the Maine coast north from the New Hampshire border to Nova Scotia, you'd travel about 225 miles. If it were possible to walk the coast between the same two points, the distance would be more than 3500 miles. New York and Los Angeles are only 2800 miles apart, and the terrain is an easier hike. There are also more than 200 offshore islands on the Maine coast, adding hundreds more miles to what many regard as the most beautiful seacoast in the world.

But if Maine is linked to the sea, there is more to it that would make it a beautiful place even without the drama of the surf pounding on granite and the spectacular storms the people there call "goose-drownders." It's a place of lush, quiet forests, with meadows carpeted with wildflowers, and sparkling blue lakes. It's dotted with tidy little towns and cities that do all they can to keep their small-town charm.

More than half of the State of Maine is wild and untouched, partly because until very recent times it was inaccessible, but mostly because of the character of the people who call the State of Maine their home.

They prefer to be called "Down-Easters," even though the finger of land they live on is clearly "up" from the rest of the continental United States. It's a term that goes back to the days when Maine was officially part of Massachusetts and the only way to get there was by sailing down the prevailing west wind.

It never was easy to get there, which may help to explain why a real Down-Easter isn't quite like other Americans. They have a reputation for being close-mouthed, for instance, and when they do speak it's in accents not quite like any other. They enjoy a good story, but most sincerely believe in the old axiom: "Laugh before breakfast, weep before supper." But if that implies they are humorless and unfriendly, the picture is not quite accurate. They are probably more like the original New Englanders than anyone living in the New England states today. They believe in thrift and hard work, they are proud of their native horse sense and their ability to survive harsh winters without resorting to the trappings of the 20th century. They believe that cleanliness is next to Godliness, and that Godliness is the most important of mankind's aspirations.

They live closer to nature than most Americans, and they live more by the values we associate with the American pioneers than anybody, including Alaskans.

They have a fierce loyalty to their state, and refer to all other Americans as "Out-of-Staters." It's not that they don't like the rest of us, but they know they have something special that the rest of us will never quite feel no matter how hard we try.

Laced with placid lakes, such as Moosehead Lake at Greenville (above), and sparkling rivers like the Penobscot (top and facing page) and the Nesowadnehunk (left) Maine is a paradise for lovers of all water sports.

West Quoddy Head Lighthouse (left) overlooks the Bay of Fundy and marks the easternmost point of the United States. Remaining pictures show buildings in the town of Milbridge, Washington County, which is as close to the wilderness as New England can be, mainly comprising almost untraveled forests and lakes.

Among the first summer visitors to Bar Harbor (these pages) were artists attracted by the area's outstanding natural beauty.

Main picture and inset below: the attractive lobstering and fishing village of Beals Island. Remaining insets: Bar Harbor, Mount Desert Island's main town, has been a popular vacation resort for over a century and offers modern hotels as well as old inns and shops. 100-foot private yachts moor alongside little fishing boats in Northeast Harbor (overleaf) which, among other attractions, offers daily whale and seabird watching cruises.

Southwest Harbor (right and insets) was planned by Sir Francis Bernard, the last English governer of Massachusetts, in 1792 and has since grown into a town of some 2,000 inhabitants. Seal Harbor (remaining pictures) lies in the southern part of Mount Desert Island's eastern peninsula and is the terminal for the ferry that serves the Cranberry Isles and Southwest Harbor. Overleaf: Northeast Harbor, considered to be among the most beautiful and best maintained ports on the east coast, is the summer home and stop-over point for thousands of sailing and power yachts from around the world.

Top: one of the Hamilton Laboratory Farm Buildings in Acadia National Park. Main picture and right, inset: the imposing Bass Harbor Head Light, on Mount Desert Island. The rich forests of Maine provided building material for the earliest settlers' attractive homes, some of which still stand (remaining pictures).

South of Stonington lies the little-visited Isle Au Haut (above) pronounced "eeloho," part of which belongs to Acadia National Park. To the east lies Great Duck Island, with its wild, craggy shore (left inset) and coastal station (top and right inset). Left: a typical Maine coastal scene.

Stonington (these pages and overleaf) is a pretty town with timber piers and multicolored houses scattered around the famous pink granite rocks that, between 1885 and 1925, supported a thriving quarrying industry. This "granite boom" attracted Italians and other immigrants who brought an interesting cultural mix to the town, whose other prosperous industry was fishing, lobster being the most important catch. Today, thanks to harbor improvements and a new fish pier, together with an increased demand in building materials, both industries are enjoying a revival.

In 1846 a fort was erected at Bucksport (right and above) during a boundary dispute with Britain. War never came, but in the earlier War of 1812 the British captured two forts near Castine (top). Overleaf: Fort Knox, overlooking Penobscot Bay, is Maine's largest fort and a National Historic Landmark. The past is also remembered in the Penobscot Museum (top inset) and the graceful white clapboard buildings of Castine (bottom inset).

PERKINS-BROOKS HOUSE
1780

A variety of sailing craft fills the harbor of Camden (these pages), but the town is best known as the home of Maine's windjammer fleet, the country's largest concentration of passenger-carrying schooners, which have been taking tourists on sailing trips since the 1930s.

There is much charm in Owl's Head, with its secluded bay (main picture right) and somewhat untidy antique store (above). Top inset and below: colorful scenes at Camden. Bottom inset: the fascinating interior of Mathews Museum of Maine in Union, which includes examples of coopering, cobbling, farm tools and allied equipment.

WOODEN PLOW
ABOUT
1800

At the tip of the St. George Peninsula is Port Clyde (these pages and previous page left inset), a small fishing village which, despite its quiet, unassuming character, is steeped in history. Here Waymouth captured his Indians, N.C. Wyeth painted and Samuel Champlain sailed. Boat building and lobstering are the major activities of Friendship (previous page, remaining pictures), a charming, natural seaport made famous by the annual Friendship Sloop Race, a three-day regatta where vintage sloops as well as present-day models compete.

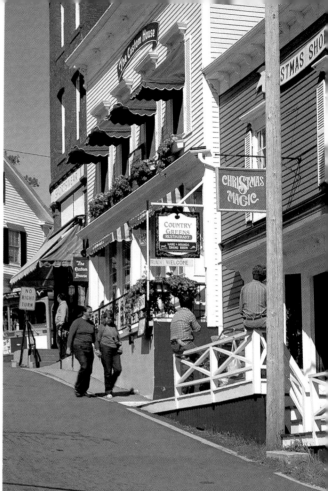

Enticing shops line the crooked streets of
Boothbay Harbor (top right and left). Fort
William Henry (above) is allegedly New England's
first stone fort. Right: a house on stilts in
South Bristol. Facing page: Pemaquid Lighthouse,
perched on the craggy promontory that juts out
into the waters of Muscongus Bay.

Boothbay Harbor (these pages) is the liveliest of Maine's mid-coast resorts, offering high quality shopping, eating and even night life. The town is perhaps best known for its sailing facilities and enjoys the title "boating capital of New England."

As with many of Maine's coastal towns, shipbuilding and sailing were the prime industries in Boothbay Harbor (these pages) until the early years of this century. Today this quaint, well preserved town, with its outlying communities, plays host to the tourists who flock here in the summer months.

Boats are still built, repaired and sold at
Boothbay Harbor (these pages and overleaf).
Today, however, the industry focuses largely on
sailing as a sport and tourist activity, which
brings much revenue to the area during the summer,
and especially on Windjammer Days, when the harbor
is filled with dozens of passenger-carrying
schooners and hundreds of smaller sailing craft.

SEA HAG
BOOTHBAY HARBOR

IRIS

Fort Edgecomb (above) dates back to 1808 and was built to protect Wiscasset (remaining pictures), which was then the most important shipping centre north of Boston. Situated fourteen miles from the open sea, this charming town has one of Maine's deepest harbors and, as the abundance of fine sea captains' mansions indicate, must have prospered greatly from its once-thriving port. A strong sense of its maritme history is retained by the wrecks of two ancient wooden ships – the *Hesper* and the *Luther Little* – which have come to rest on the Sheepscot River.

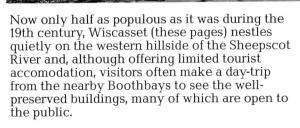

Now only half as populous as it was during the 19th century, Wiscasset (these pages) nestles quietly on the western hillside of the Sheepscot River and, although offering limited tourist accomodation, visitors often make a day-trip from the nearby Boothbays to see the well-preserved buildings, many of which are open to the public.

Perched on the banks of the Kennebec River, Augusta, a relatively small city of some 22,000 inhabitants, is the capital of Maine. The town's first permanent building, Fort Western (top and above), was built in 1754 and now serves as a museum. On one of the busiest stretches of the Kennebec River is the distinguished red brick city of Bath (remaining pictures), where the famous Iron Works became a shipbuilding site in 1889 and is now one of the largest producers of Navy ships in the nation.

Augusta's State Capitol Building (right and facing page), designed by Charles Bulfinch, has doubled in size since completion in 1832, and now sports a new 185-foot dome. Above and top: Gardiner, a pretty town roughly five miles downriver from Augusta.

The coastline north of Portland is broken into many islands and peninsulas. A ferry leaves (main picture left) for Chebeague Island; (top inset and above) houses at Orrs Island and (top) South Freeport. Remaining pictures: Biddeford Pool in Saco Bay. Overleaf: the popular resort of Kennebunkport, with (right inset) the "Desert of Maine" near Freeport and (left inset) Portland Head Lighthouse.

In autumn, glorious red and gold hues enhance views of Maine's buildings, from the pale timber of Bethel church (right), to the dark, old stone church of York (facing page). Woodland scenes are also transformed (remaining pictures), especially where there is water, such as that of the Androscoggin River (overleaf), to reflect the bright colors.

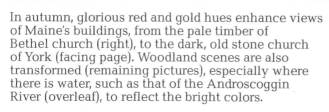